# CHUFFED AS
# A BADGER

# The funniest Ian
# Holloway quotes!

### by Gordon Law

Printed in Europe and the USA

ISBN: 9781729335987
Imprint: Independently published

Photo courtesy of: Ramzi Musallam

# Contents

# Introduction

Football has always been a serious game, so you need colourful characters to lighten the mood – and they don't come much bigger than Ian Holloway.

The outspoken Bristolian boss has not only managed a number of entertaining teams and taken Blackpool and Crystal Palace to the Premier League.

But he is also loved by the fans for his gift of the gab, with his engaging press conferences and post-match interviews often a highlight of the footballing week.

The cheeky chappy is in a league of his own when it comes to a witty one-liner, a quirky comparison or a raucous rant. Holloway is a masterful manager and comedy genius.

Famous for his analogies, surely the most memorable was when he compared a scrappy QPR win against Chesterfield to taking an ugly girl home in a taxi.

Talking about his rough luck, Holloway once complained: "If I fell in a barrel of boobs I'd come out sucking my thumb."

He's spoken on Cristiano Ronaldo's manhood, Joey Barton's backside, described David Beckham as "just a good footballer with a famous bird" and has also wanted to bark like a dog!

These classic sound bites and many more can be found in the biggest collection of Holloway quotations and I hope you laugh as much reading this book as I did in compiling it.

**Gordon Law**

# CHUFFED AS A BADGER

# CAN YOU MANAGE?

"I'm just trying to talk in a way so people don't think I'm funny anymore, I'm fed up with that. I'm not a comedian, I'm a football manager."

**The Palace boss wants to be taken seriously**

"I've got to get Dan Shittu ready for the Stoke game. I've told him to go to Iceland and ask if he can sit in one of their freezers."

**He wasn't sure if there were enough ice packs for his giant QPR defender**

"We are not instant coffee here – this is long term and I want to help lift our brand even higher."

**After signing a new contract at QPR**

## Can You Manage?

"You can ask my wife what time I finish and what time I start. She'll tell you. Last night it was half past 12, watching clips."

**The Palace manager is always working**

"It looked like I had a terrible limp, dragging one leg behind me like something out of The Terminator."

**The Tangerines boss struggles with a game of beach football**

"Let's hope me and the players can have a decent marriage."

**Holloway wants love at Palace**

## CHUFFED AS A BADGER

"As a father I've been tough at times – I took my son's four things he loved in his bedroom once. He had to behave himself to get them back, one a month. He was 13 and was misbehaving in class at school and wasn't fulfilling his ability. My dad wouldn't have put up with that. I think it was his music centre, television, games console and a Nintendo Game Boy. How harsh am I? But how bad was that for me at 50 years old? To be detached at Man United – did I deserve it? My wife will tell you I did."

**On having to watch Palace from the stands at Old Trafford after being banned from the dugout for yelling abuse at the referee**

## Can You Manage?

"After my chairman's shot a few birds, I'll see if he can get me some players."

**Holloway takes a pot shot at his Blackpool chairman**

"Did we know we were going to spend that much? No. The chairman was like a kid in a sweet shop."

**Holloway on Palace chief Steve Parish**

"When it comes to looks, my wife's got a lot more about her."

**The Tangerines manager is punching above his weight**

"I'd pack in. I can't work for this madness. I would resign. They do not know what they're talking about."

**The Blackpool boss blasts the Premier League and says he will step down as manager if the Tangerines are punished for playing a weakened team against Villa**

"Do you believe everything you read in The Sun? They've got some nice tits in that paper."

**The QPR boss was asked about reports linking him with the vacant Millwall job**

"This is our cave, and I like living in it."

**Holloway on remaining at Loftus Road**

"I'm sick and tired of every Tom, Dick and Harry getting linked with my job every day. Well ding, dang, do. It's my job, I own it and it's up to anyone else to take it off me."

**He is feeling under pressure at QPR**

"We've got to be solid and horrible to break down, I don't want to be southern softies!"

**Holloway on QPR's tougher attitude**

"One minute I was painting the lounge, the next I'm being asked to manage a Championship side. My wife will have to finish the glossing."

**On getting back into management with Blackpool**

"I know I've got a few chickens but it is ridiculous to link me with that. It is absolute rubbish."

**The Blackpool manager dismisses reports linking him with the job at Blackburn who are owned by an Indian poultry firm**

"It's very rare I get down. You can put too much emphasis on the wrong things. I've a great friend I talk to who is a farmer. Some of the things he has to do, something breaks and he fixes them. It's just amazing."

**The Palace boss gets philosophical**

"It's still in my body and I'll have to pass it at some time but my passing's absolutely diabolical. That's what I told the doctor, 'What chance have I got of passing anything – did you see me play?' When it happened I was lying on the floor of my office in pain thinking this place isn't very clean – the carpet needs changing, the walls needs painting... and when I got up I was covered in rubbish. If I want to be in the Premier League one day, I should be able to roll around in agony on my floor without getting dirty. So I'm going to order a new carpet and some paint for my office. There's always something good that comes out of something bad."

**The Plymouth manager is suffering with back trouble**

## CHUFFED AS A BADGER

"I believe I could sell a fridge to an Eskimo."

**The Palace boss is the expert salesman**

"I took them orienteering on Monday – and two of them got lost. We had to go out in a van to get them. I can't tell you who they are because they are a little embarrassed."

**On a QPR pre-season trip to Scotland**

"The club isn't on solid ground. It's like I'm on a block of ice. I don't know whether I'm going through it, or slide off."

**The manager on coming in to QPR**

"Tony, can I ring you back? I'm just doing an interview, mate you've ruined it. I'm fined now. I'm fined. I'm fined. Alright mate, I'll ring you back. Thanks."

**Holloway takes a call from boss Tony Fernandes and breaks a club rule for allowing a phone to ring during interviews**

"So what does the future bring for Ian Holloway? Well, I've only been out of football for a few days, but I already feel like a man who has been stranded on a desert island. As the character played by Tom Hanks in the film Castaway said, 'I'll just wait to see what the tide brings in'."

**After leaving the Palace job**

"I haven't sworn for almost a week now. When I saw a film of my sortie into the centre circle at the final whistle, I could quite clearly see myself mouth a number of obscenities at the referee. And I was ashamed of myself. That was why I accepted the FA's charge of improper conduct and paid a £2,000 fine. In fact, my behaviour cost me a grand total of £2,012 – because I also had to pay a £12 'fine' to my wife Kim after initially telling her that I hadn't sworn."

**The Eagles boss had an expensive week**

"They said I lost the changing room. I know where it is, it's down the corridor on the left."

**The Palace manager hits back at critics**

"We did a scam television programme. This fella was brought in to training, allegedly called Eduardo and Latvia's captain. We told the players a rich guy had just bought the club and wanted him in his team. He was cack, absolutely useless. But I said it was out of my hands and they had to give him a chance. And they fell for it. After 10 minutes of training the lads were booting him up in the air. It was really funny."

**Holloway brought in a fake player to a QPR training session for a practical joke**

"I've got to knock that horrible smell out of my boys because they smell of complacency."

**Holloway on his stinky Plymouth team**

# CHUFFED AS A BADGER

"I am stressed to hell – not when I watch my team, not when I'm out on the grass coaching, but just trying to say 'Who's this? Where has he come from? What's his name? How do you spell it?'"

**On watching other teams' players**

"It's like when I was a kid waiting for Santa to turn up, worried whether I'd been good enough. To then see he has and he's given you a few toys – this is even better than that feeling. That excitement and exhilaration when you open the door and can see the presents – this is even better."

**Holloway on the joys of promotion**

"The club has galloped forward and I want to try and bring it back a little bit. If we are a horse, we are not a race horse, we are a horse that is going to try and pull a cart and make sure everybody is on it. I don't want to gallop off and look all lovely with shiny shoes on saying 'look at me'. That's not what we are. We are an old cob of a fella that is going to drag everybody with us."

**He horses around on his return as QPR boss**

"I am more than happy [at Blackpool] and I am afraid the chairman will need a hell of a tub of cream to get rid of me – I'm like a bad rash and not easily curable."

**On speculation he is willing to leave the Tangerines**

"I love Blackpool. We're very similar. We both look better in the dark."

**Holloway is enjoying it with the Tangerines**

"Statistically, I'm currently the worst Leicester manager in history and that doesn't sit well with me. On my gravestone it will say, 'Here lies Ollie – he tried'. I will never give up."

**The Leicester boss always gives 110 per cent**

"If we did get in the play-offs, I'd be singing and dancing but it would be a horrible song as I can't sing a note!"

**The QPR boss is honest as the day is long**

"We're 5-0 down with a minute to go on this one."

**A frustrated Ian Holloway on trying to bring Middlesbrough's Andrew Davies to QPR but he apparently wanted more money**

**Gianni Paladini:** "You f*cking bastard, I am going to kill you, you f*cking bastard... where are you, f*cking hell where are you?"

**Ian Holloway:** "I am on the toilet. My wife is in the house. Ask her."

**Paladini:** "She could be at f*cking Wolves with you."

**The QPR chief calls a virus-hit Ian Holloway after believing reports he was to join Wolves. Holloway had to reassure him in person**

"I've realised I'm hideously ugly when I don't get what I want. My dad said to me years ago, 'What's the point in arguing?' I wish I was more like Bjorn Borg – but I'm probably more like John McEnroe in temperament, but not in skill."

**The Eagles boss admits he can be stubborn**

"I am not a pair of bell bottoms. I am not a high waisted pair you had at school with the pockets so big you could get your books in. I'm not that pair of trousers. I'm getting re-tailored all the time to get in fashion because that is what you have to do, because the game is changing all the time."

**Holloway feels he has evolved as a manager on his return as QPR boss**

"It's a football club, not a prison. People shouldn't see me coming and think, 'Oh here's the b*stard'."

**He doesn't want to be feared at Leicester**

"I'm fed up with my career going backwards because my team, has been sold from underneath my nose. Before I die, I wanted to have the chance to spend some money. There was a bomb ticking and if it had gone off and somebody else had got the job I would always have felt the bridesmaid. The game, the business, stinks sometimes but I don't. I would have been a liar if I had stayed at Plymouth."

**He gives an honest assessment on why he left Plymouth for Leicester**

"If I hadn't done that programme, I wouldn't be sitting here now. Before I did it, I believed that I was a person who was kind, considerate and believed in free speech. The anger management expert showed me I was a jumped-up, obnoxious little git who wouldn't listen at home because of what happened at work. If I'd carried on the way I was, I would have destructed everything I had."

**The Plymouth manager took part in a BBC programme called The Stress Test**

"Ha ha! Well that's very flattering but I think they'll have to go and swivel on that idea!"

**On being offered the England job**

"I'm a people person and I can't wait to work with these people."

**He's a man of the people after being appointed at QPR in 2001**

"The result is sometimes in the lap of the Gods. But I will prepare to try and win the game. My record over the years has been shocking. I'm like a cheap tea bag – I don't stay long in the cup!"

**Ahead of Plymouth's tie with Peterborough**

"I got them from my father who had more sayings than you can hang your hat on."

**Holloway on his amusing turns of phrase**

## CHUFFED AS A BADGER

"I feel like I have been acting in Coronation Street all my life and now I am King Lear. I just felt I couldn't turn this down. I can't wait to get started. This is a whole new challenge which throws me into a whole new ball park."

**Holloway after taking the Leicester job**

"In football, there is no definite lifespan or time span for a manager. After a while you start smelling of fish. The other week it looked like I was stinking of Halibut!"

**After Rangers' poor start**

"He's a kitten after what I've had before."

**On Leicester chairman Milan Mandaric**

"When you're a manager, it's a case of 'have suitcase will travel' and I certainly didn't want to travel with my trousers down."

**The Plymouth manager on moving jobs**

"I've total optimism and that helps his total pessimism."

**On his Blackpool chairman Karl Oyston**

"It's easy to say after the event, 'Holloway should have done this, Holloway should have done that' but after the event and funnily enough that's when Holloway realises it as well."

**Holloway on the value of hindsight**

"You have to ask about a bar of soap at this club. I even had to pay for our pre-match meal on my own credit card on Saturday."

**Holloway on QPR's financial constraints**

**Reporter:** "Ian, have you got any injury worries?"

**Holloway:** "No, I'm fully fit, thank you."

**The Tangerines boss makes a wise crack to a journalist**

"It's a mad house in the Premiership and I'm glad I'm in it."

**The Blackpool manager is enjoying life in the top flight**

"I've had a week from hell, I'm trying to learn how to relax. I'm now going to enjoy this, take my brain out and stick it in an ice bucket."

**Holloway can take it easy after QPR's 4-1 win over Hartlepool**

"I am a football manager. I can't see into the future. Last year I thought I was going to Cornwall on my holidays but I ended up going to Lyme Regis!"

**On whether QPR could beat Man City**

"I don't like it when they call me madcap. I'm not mad and I don't wear a cap."

**The Plymouth manager hits back**

# CHUFFED AS A BADGER

# FAN
# BANTER

"I was disappointed with our fans and with their fans. I'd like to say to ours, 'You should have stayed'. Everybody who did stay, well done, you deserved that. Don't go home early. You might not have missed your last bus, but you missed a treat... And as for their fans, 'Getting sacked in the morning?' I don't think so."

**Holloway blasts both sets of fans after QPR netted two stoppage-time goals to snatch a 2-2 draw at home to Brentford**

"Twenty thousand people running the club – that's going to have to be one hell of a room they book when they hold their annual general meeting..."

**On Ebbsfleet's unique club model**

"Most of our fans get behind us and are fantastic but those who don't should shut the hell up or they can come round to my house and I will fight them."

**His ultimatum to the Rangers fans**

"I didn't like the banter to be honest. I don't think that's respectful. How many times do we as human beings turn a blind eye to things? It's not right is it? It ain't funny is it?"

**The Millwall boss fumes at Lions fans who made 'obscene' chants about Jimmy Savile**

"Apparently it's my fault that the Titanic sank."

**On criticism from Plymouth supporters**

"I want to try and spread the support with my Bristol connection. Rovers are in the bottom division so why can't I try and convert some of them into Argyle fans? We're in the West Country so it's not that far away. Only two and a half hours away in a slow car, an hour-and-a half in a fast one – or 10 minutes in a rocket! As long as you aimed it right, you'd be down here really quickly. Don't land it on the pitch, though, because you'd ruin it!"

**He wants Rovers fans to watch Plymouth**

"Some of the songs our fans were singing, I found myself chuckling. I can't wait to hear what they come up with on Sunday."

**Holloway enjoys the Palace chants**

# Fan Banter

"I went to Southampton the other week, with Kim. These kids shouted, 'Oh Holloway, you're a legend. Sign this'. Then they said, 'Thanks, Steve'. It was the same in the Chinese chip shop when I was at Bristol Rovers. They started off by calling me 'Horroway'. But before long it was, 'Salt and vinegar, Steve? How much you earn, Steve?' Why is it always Steve?"

**Ian 'Steve' Holloway**

"If I'd have been one of their fans I'd have hit him with a bottle myself."

**The Plymouth boss after a wild goal celebration by Hasney Aljofree led to objects being thrown by Peterborough fans**

# CHUFFED AS A BADGER

# OFF THE PITCH

# CHUFFED AS A BADGER

"I wouldn't wear one myself. I think you look a bit of a ponce... I wouldn't wear gloves and I certainly wouldn't wear one of those things around my neck. DJ does it but his is a cut-off hat."

**Holloway laughs at his players' efforts to keep warm by wearing snoods**

"One of the lads said, 'Oh, I can remember the days when I used to buy my suits from Burton's' and I was thinking, 'Christ! I've got one at home I got from Asda!' I hadn't progressed as far as Burton's yet."

**On the culture shock on arriving as a player at QPR in the 1990/91 season**

"I went out for a meal with my good lady to a wonderful Indian restaurant down here and we had a bottle of champagne. I didn't buy her any flowers because she didn't want any. She was lucky she didn't go to the opticians so she can see what I really look like! I always keep her away from there. Every time she wants to go to the opticians I say, 'No, you don't need to go in there, love!' and turn and walk the other way."

**The Plymouth boss on his dear wife**

"I've got four lovely horses and I would have a terrible problem eating horse meat."

**The Palace manager on the 2013 horse meat scandal**

## CHUFFED AS A BADGER

"Sir David Beckham? You're having a laugh. He's just a good footballer with a famous bird. Can you imagine if Posh was called Lady Beckham? We'd never hear the end of it!"

**Holloway on reports about a possible knighthood for David Beckham**

"I need a bigger garden. I only had a little one. I told my wife after a week I was knackered. I tried to help by pulling out weeds and it turned out they were her plants! She wasn't very happy!"

**He upsets the wife while on gardening leave at Rangers**

"I was a bit worried no one was going to turn up at my book signing. I was relieved to see some people there. I thought about sitting outside Northern Rock because there would be a queue there."

**Holloway thought of a novel way to get more fans at his book launch**

"I was never tempted to become a punk. I was Sidney Serious, I was into George Benson. I was smooth. Smooth as a cashmere codpiece."

**The Plymouth manager on his music preferences**

"Tell the WAGs we've got a brand new shopping centre in Plymouth."

**He wants to attract new talent to the club**

"Chuffed to beans I made it through the three hours without fainting or crying. The pain was definitely worth it, pictures to follow."

**Holloway is given a tattoo by his son Will, who is a trained artist**

"I like Oddjob, remember him? He was the sidekick of somebody. I like the way he threw that hat and knocked the thing off."

**The Plymouth boss on his favourite Bond villain**

"I've got four women in my house – my wife and my three daughters – and I tell you what, it's pretty scary. I keep my head down and if we're out shopping I try and look in a man's shop while they make their minds up."

**The Plymouth manager is surrounded by women**

"If you go to the ballet you have about eight intervals – it's different class. In fact you could almost have your 10 pints during the breaks and by the end of it you're loving it. I strongly recommend it."

**The Plymouth boss enjoys a bit of ballet**

## CHUFFED AS A BADGER

"Grease... What a great movie. When Olivia Neutron Bomb comes on in that tight gear at the end, it's scary isn't it? When she changes from nice little Sandy into a hellcat on legs... whoah! Unbelievable."

**The Plymouth manager on one of his favourite films**

"I've never had a bet myself; I wouldn't know how to put one on. I've never seen a rich gambler and I've never seen a broke bookie either. I want to become addicted to a lot of things, but not gambling. I'm addicted to my wife, though – I can't leave her alone!"

**Holloway loves his wife**

**Q:** "How much did you earn as a player, compared to Wayne Rooney?"

**A:** "Not enough to go to brothels."

**The QPR boss after Rooney admitted to having sex with prostitutes**

"If I was in there I wouldn't try to be everybody's friend. I'd have to say, 'Excuse me, hang on a minute, I think you're wrong there. Don't raise your voice at her like that, don't get like that. It's just an Oxo cube, we got it wrong and we're all in this together'. It's like the Witches of Eastwick. They need Jack Nicholson to come in and sort them right out."

**The Plymouth boss gets behind bullied Big Brother contestant Shipla Shetty**

## CHUFFED AS A BADGER

"I would like nothing more than to be like the rest of my family and chill out over Christmas, have a nice little snooze in the afternoon, eat a little bit too much, drink the odd thing that is a bit 'ooh wait a minute' then on Boxing Day watch a lovely film on the telly – Chitty Chitty Bang or something – and have a game of charades."

**Ahead of Plymouth's Christmas schedule**

"I mean no respect to Donatella [Versace]. I'm sure she would not be flattered to hear she looks like Marc Bircham."

**Holloway reckons his QPR midfielder bears a resemblance to the fashion designer**

"She takes more tablets than Moses climbing the mountain and I swear I can hear her rattle when she walks. But she's 74 and an absolute star – and she still works at a chemist in Bristol, which is quite handy because she's also their best customer!"

**The Plymouth boss on his mother**

"I watched Hamlet the other night and, what a shame, they nearly all died in the end. I've never heard so many words make so little sense. It was brilliant, a bit like my interviews."

**Holloway steps in for Germaine Greer on the Late Review panel**

"I've ridden a horse but I'm rubbish at it. I look like a crab sat on a horse with my hunched back. I've got rounded shoulders so I'm in all sorts of trouble and the bloody horse seems to know it as well! Many a time my wife's seen me in excruciating agony when I've gone down instead of going up – let's just say those bloody saddles are rather hard."

**The Plymouth manager would never make it as a cowboy**

"There was a woman in it who was quite well-endowed and two boys who used to get drunk and have a fight – it had everything for me."

**The Plymouth boss on Dukes of Hazzard**

"I think us human beings will end up with thumbs like giant crabs pretty soon because of all the texting that goes on and the playing of these stupid computer games and we'll have lost the art of talking. It really does worry me."

**Plymouth's manager is concerned with modern technology**

"You think when you've seen one penguin – you've seen them all. But this place was amazing. There were thousands of them. It was a brilliant sight. God! Wandering among them was breathtaking; I'll never forget it."

**The Millwall manager enjoyed his holiday to Lundy Island**

# CHUFFED AS A BADGER

# PLAYER POWER

"The doctor grafted a bit of Danny's hamstring onto his knee, but that won't be a problem for him. He's got more hamstring than the rest of the squad put together."

**Holloway marvels at Shittu's large thighs**

"[Enrique] De Lucas' pedigree is unbelievable. If he were a dog, he'd win Crufts."

**He is a fan of his Blackpool player**

"I know everyone screams that he should play in the middle and I'm no nugget! I know what job he can do there."

**On playing Richard Langley in a central position for QPR**

"Have you ever seen The Incredibles? They have a kid and he's just so quick, like 'whoosh' and he's gone, and they call him Dash. And I think Mr Incredible looks like Iain Dowie."
**On Scott Sinclair, then on loan at Plymouth, and fellow manager Dowie**

"Paul Furlong is my vintage Rolls Royce and he cost me nothing. We polish him, look after him and I have him fine-tuned by my mechanics. We take good care of him because we have to drive him every day, not just save him for weddings."
**Holloway wants to keep his veteran QPR forward motoring**

"When my wife first saw Marc for the first time, she said he was a fine specimen of a man. She says I have nothing to worry about, but I think she wants me to buy her a QPR shirt with his name on the back for Christmas."

**Is Ian Holloway a little threatened by QPR striker Marc Nygaard?**

"He's played 150 games for us and that was his first-ever goal. Believe it or not, I said to him at half-time, 'Are you ever going to score a goal for us?' And he laughed and said, 'Yeah, one day I will!' Within 10 minutes of the restart, he scored – unbelievable!"

**After Paul Connolly finally netted for Plymouth**

"He's been out for a year and Richard Langley is still six months away from being Richard Langley, and I could do with a fully fit Richard Langley."

**Holloway on his Hoops midfielder**

"[George Santos] is a big lad. He can clean out your guttering without standing on a ladder."

**Holloway thinks his QPR player could make some money on the side**

"What a complete chicken nugget with double barbecue sauce he is."

**On Plymouth defender Paul Connolly**

"He's the quickest thing we've got, and an absolute animal."

**The QPR boss admires Danny Shittu's speed**

"I call him Ronseal, he does exactly what it says on the tin. He's an out-and-out winger. He can turn, he can beat people and he makes the right choice nearly every time."

**After on-loan winger Jerome Thomas netted the winner for QPR at Swindon**

"What we've all got to do is pick him up, slap him around and make him feel welcome."

**The QPR boss helps the homesick Doudou**

"It's been embarrassing, he's won every award. He won Groundsman of the Year and Young Player of the Year – even at the age of 37!"

**Holloway on Paul Furlong winning all of QPR's end-of-season honours**

"Gareth Ainsworth is the most physical winger I've seen. He calls himself the wolf man because of his sideburns but I don't pick fault with hairdos if players perform."

**Holloway praises his midfielder's hair**

"I'll keep signing him till he's nearly 50 or 60 if he keeps putting the ball in the net."

**The Palace boss on 'old man' Kevin Phillips**

# CHUFFED AS A BADGER

"Barry Hayles had a top on today that made him look like a traffic light. I don't know what the matter is with him."

**The Leicester manager on his striker's unusual fashion sense**

"[Josh] Scowen should have been sent off, it's an absolutely scandalous tackle in my opinion. I'm going to hammer him. He got angry because they were playing around us. Well you've got to take your medicine son, don't kick out at someone like that."

**The Hoops boss blasts a tackle... by his own player after a 4-0 defeat at Hull City**

"Everyone calls him a gypsy but I can assure you he doesn't live in a caravan. He has a house with foundations."

**On long-haired QPR defender Gino Padula**

"Hasney's bust his hooter. He can smell round corners now."

**On Plymouth defender Hasney Aljofree's facial injury**

"If I said he couldn't play I think he would kill me, literally."

**The Blackpool boss is scared to leave out Charlie Adam against Manchester United**

# CHUFFED AS A BADGER

# MANAGING JUST FINE

"We've talked him into the right type of boiler that won't break."

**Holloway's message to Blackpool chairman Karl Oyston after the players had to suffer with cold showers**

"He says they're feeding off scraps. I think we are waiting for their scraps to fall off the table and then chew them."

**Holloway on how far Blackpool are behind Premier League rivals Stoke**

"Over the years, QPR have been a bit of a flitty, farty, we-like-a-fancy-Dan-footballer club."

**Holloway wants more grounded players**

"We will have to be slightly different away from home, but part of our game is drawing teams onto us and then knocking them out with a [sucker] punch. I don't think we are going to be a Sugar Ray Leonard, I think we are going to be more of a Muhammad Ali against Joe Frasier."

**The Palace boss on boxing to victory**

"We will need everyone at Selhurst Park pulling in the right direction and not just the players. We need the directors, the kit man, the programme sellers and the tea lady all in it together."

**Holloway wants togetherness at Palace**

"The dietician is going to get rid of that when he comes in. Although, first, we've got to get a dietician. That's one of the things on my list."

**Blackpool will have to stop eating biscuits and fish and chips after victories**

"I'd rather do that than build chicken sheds no one wanted!"

**After Blackpool reached the Championship play-offs in 2009. Holloway had spent a year out of the game building hen houses**

"I call us the orange club – because our future's bright!"

**Holloway has high hopes for QPR**

"Someone with a budget of our size can stand up for the man in the street, smash these big people in the face and say: 'Have that!'"
**On the challenge of keeping Blackpool up**

"We are not even David if this league is Goliath, we are smaller than him. And we haven't even got a slingshot."
**Holloway on his Blackpool underdogs ahead of their match against Liverpool**

"I want to win the Champions League in two years. Well, that's as wild a dream as us being in the Premier League."
**He sets the bar high for Blackpool**

"Our castle was made of sand, but there is concrete underneath."

**He is confident Blackpool can bounce back after relegation from the Premier League**

"At the minute, the dish we're making tastes lovely, like one of those puddings on MasterChef. It won't take much for it to burn or go soggy, but their focus is awesome. They are getting it just right."

**The Palace manager is cooking up a treat**

"If the club was a chocolate bar, it would have licked itself."

**On QPR's time in the top flight**

"Dream on! If they want to insult me by only offering £3.5million and then get it all over the paper and try to upset me. Well, sorry, they're barking up the wrong tree, they're messing with the wrong dog and I'll come and bite them."

**The Blackpool boss on insulting offers for Charlie Adam**

"When my mum was running our house, when I was a kid, all the money was put into tins. She knew what was in every tin and I know how much I've got in my tin – that's the way we'll run this club."

**Holloway won't spend money that Rangers don't have**

"Our shop's never closed. We're like a Kwik-E-Mart."

**Holloway is frustrated Blackpool are unable to shut up shop**

"This really is squeaky-bum time, and we have all got to show that we've got the bottle to come through it."

**Pinching Sir Alex Ferguson's famous quote, he is keeping his nerve at Palace**

"I'm just happy to get one over Mrs Doubtfire [Warnock] but fair play to him – he's done wonders for Palace."

**The Leicester boss on his managerial rival**

"Wilfried Zaha might be out for about six months to stop you from talking about him all the time. Get my message do you? I should hope so. That's probably Arsene Wenger on the phone now. Knowing you lot, it would be and there'll be some sort of story about it. For Christ sakes, write about something else. He's going to be out for months and months. Why should I give you a straight answer? I'm sick and fed up about reading about him. If it happens, it happens, if it don't, it don't. Try and get other stories. And as for your little programme on the telly where you're counting down, just go and get a job, get a life. However many days and however many hours are left till this stupid, pathetic window that forces people to have to do things is just... not very good is it?"

**He rants at the press over Zaha's future**

"QPR is the people's club and everybody can have a piece of that pie. A pie that's already smelling beautifully."

**Holloway likes a pie**

"As Fairground Attraction said, 'It's got to be... perfect!'"

**The Blackpool manager's goal is written in song**

"When QPR seemed to be dying, we were a carcass and the vultures came and fed off our bones."

**Holloway on having to sell his players**

"We had our Christmas party at Crystal Palace during the week – and I am happy to report that my directors didn't ask me to copy Blackburn boss Henning Berg by dressing up to do a song and dance routine."

**On celebrating the festivities at Palace**

"It's about bedding this group in and making sure that they know how to speak to each other and what's acceptable. Anyone with more than one dog, when you introduce another one, you get a few problems."

**On bedding new Palace players into the squad**

"When we go to Fulham I'll take a little hacksaw, smuggle the statue on the bus and take it home with me."

**Holloway has a cunning plan to steal Fulham's statue of Michael Jackson**

"I'm all geared up for the Derby game. I'm looking forward to it although it's raining heavily down here at the moment. I haven't quite finished my ark yet, so it's a bit worrying. But we've got our water rings and a rubber ring ready and Derby don't know about that so we've got one up on them already."

**The Plymouth manager ahead of a wet FA Cup tie**

"I'll offer him a glass of white wine as I know he
likes red."

**Holloway gets the booze in ahead of Sir
Alex Ferguson's visit to Blackpool**

"We've got Leicester on Saturday and they've
sacked Martin Allen, their manager, which was
a bit of a strange state of affairs – especially
after they'd just beaten Watford 4-1. That'll
teach him!"

**The Plymouth boss on management perils**

"If he's only worth £4million, then I'm a
Scotsman called McTavish."

**Holloway on bids received for Charlie Adam**

"I don't think he would get his left toe out of bed for the wages we would pay for him."

**On looking to sign Sergei Rebrov**

"If someone wants to pay me £50million for my house I'll bloody sell it to him."

**Holloway knows that money talks**

"If some bright spark from the Premier League, or Barclays Premier League as we're supposed to call it, wants to come down and have a chat and a cup of coffee... you'll probably get it chucked in your lap."

**On claims he could be fined for fielding a weakened Blackpool team against Villa**

"When I was at Bristol Rovers, there was a journalist who wrote a match report where he said that if Bristol City had my two strikers – who, in that game, were rubbish – then City would be a team Bristol could be proud of. Oooof! I got him to the training ground. He didn't know why. I said, 'You are going to apologise to my team, you b*stard'. I sat all my players down. I had the two centre halves stand up. I said, 'Right, now tell these two – who you only gave five out of 10 each – just how well you think they played, you a*shole'."

**Holloway takes a reporter to task and stands up for his underappreciated defenders**

"I went swimming with my players but my trunks were so tight that I got called a budgie-smuggler."

**The Plymouth manager had the mickey taken out of him**

"If we get [a first home win] against Man City, it would be absolutely laughable. Look at them donkey-lashers – go on! The fans aren't going to accept that because you have just been beaten by Blackpool – that bunch down there, them Seasiders, that tangerine mob."

**The Blackpool manager on facing the might of Manchester City**

"I might be in a bit of a Skoda garage rather than a Mercedes garage, but I am telling you some old bangers don't half polish up great."

**On claims his Blackpool squad is one of the cheapest ever in the Premier League**

"Why would I sell him and why would he want to go to a club like that? They strut around as if they are a big club, but they ain't. Southampton have come in twice now and I've told them to p*ss off both times. They won't be coming back, I can promise you."

**The Plymouth boss on Southampton trying to unsettle David Norris**

# CHUFFED AS A BADGER

# A FUNNY OLD GAME

## CHUFFED AS A BADGER

"I watched Arsenal in the Champions League the other week playing some of the best football I've ever seen and yet they couldn't have scored in a brothel with two grand in their pockets."

**Plymouth's boss on Arsenal's bad finishing**

"As a player, Roy Keane was awesome – and as hard as nails. You wouldn't mess with him. A running machine, a tackling machine – a winning machine. He was like a shark in the middle of the pitch. There was nothing of him but if you clattered into him it was like hitting the side of a train. I just couldn't live with him."

**The Plymouth boss hails the United great**

"I need to go shopping most weeks. I run out of milk, I run out of eggs, I run out of bread, I need to get a paper. But you can't do that, can you? If you're the Premier League team and the window's closed and you run out of centre forwards, and you ain't got any left, you can't go shopping until the window opens again. And then there's a mad rush in January. So all you lot wait until there's a mad rush and you start speculating on who's done any good in that window and before it closes you're all talking about them. The little bloke with his little machine – how boring is it? Let's turn over and see some real life. Why do you put speculation on things when it hasn't happened yet? If it happens, then great we'll tell you about it. But in the meantime, what about the rest of my team?"

**Holloway slams the media and transfer window**

"It was a bit cheeky wasn't it? But I don't think it was that bad. It would have been worse if he'd turned round and dropped the front of his shorts instead. I don't think there's anything wrong with a couple of butt cheeks personally... If anybody's offended by seeing a backside, get real. Maybe they're just jealous that he's got a real nice tight one, with no cellulite or anything."

**The Plymouth boss on Manchester City's Joey Barton mooning Everton fans**

"Neil Warnock has been an inspiration to me. But sometimes on the line me and him do clash a little bit."

**The Eagles boss on his contemporary**

"There's about as much chance of re-signing DJ Campbell as there is of me wearing high heels and calling myself Sheila."

**Holloway dismisses reports the striker is coming back to Blackpool**

"I'm not tempted to put the boots on again, ever. But then Hessie's a lot fitter than I am. He never used to be but he is now. We should check him to make sure he's not an alien because that bloke's just superhuman. I reckon if you cut him up the middle there's going to be a little alien holding up a stick like on Men in Black! Steward's inquiry on Andy Hessenthaler – is he human?"

**On Andy Hessenthaler playing, aged 42**

"I think he's an absolutely fantastic bloke, top geezer. And if he wants to carry a little horse on the side of the pitch, I don't care."

**On Stuart Pearce's lucky mascot Beanie**

"My missus has this theory about penalties, and hates me when I shout, 'That was a stonewall penalty!' That isn't given. 'No, it wasn't' she says, 'because the referee never gave it'. The trouble is she's right, of course."

**Holloway is put straight by his wife**

"If the ball were a woman she'd be spending the night with [Dimitar] Berbatov."

**He praises the skillful Bulgarian**

"I tell you another crazy, crazy, crazy rule. We want women to come to football don't we? I think they're bloody pretty – a damn sight prettier than any bloke I've seen. You talk to women about footballers and what do they like – they like legs and our shorts are getting longer. We should go back to the days when half your a*se was hanging out. Why can't you let players lift up their shirts? Who is it disrespecting? What's wrong with letting a load of young ladies see a good-looking lad take his shirt off? They'd have to watch other teams, though – because my team is as ugly as hell."

**Ian Holloway talks about football shorts**

"He's Toad of Toad Hall, isn't he?"

**On Avram Grant's lookalike**

"My arms withered and my body was covered with puss-like sores, but no matter how bad it got, I consoled myself by remembering that I wasn't a Chelsea fan."

**Holloway on QPR's local rivals**

"In football you need to have everything in your cake mix to make the cake taste right. One little bit of ingredient that Tony [Pulis] uses in his cake gets talked about all the time is Rory's [Delap] throw. Call that cinnamon and he's got a cinnamon flavoured cake. It's not fair and it's not right and it's only a small part of what he does."

**Blackpool's Holloway says there is more to Stoke's style than throw-ins**

"I heard he had a twin and he ate him, but he's just brilliant."

**On AFC Wimbledon's Adebayo Akinfenwa**

"I rung Kenny Jacket straight away to congratulate him on getting Swansea promoted and he said, 'I'm waiting to get my goalie out of jail'. You can't even celebrate these days, can you?"

**Swansea's jubilant Willy Gueret was arrested at the end of their game at Bury**

"I know he was a good player, but he ain't good at what he does. In fact he is useless, you can quote me on that."

**On UEFA president Michel Platini**

"I think it's a pile of donkey dung. FIFA should scrap the Bosman ruling and get back to the way it was where anybody who is out of contract should be owned by the club and he should be able to command a fee for them."

**Holloway is frustrated with defender Tony Capaldi who wants to leave the club**

"He's six foot something, fit as a flea, good looking – he's got to have something wrong with him. Hopefully he's hung like a hamster – that would make us all feel better. Having said that, my missus has got a pet hamster at home, and his c*ck's massive."

**The Blackpool boss is a big admirer of Cristiano Ronaldo**

## A Funny Old Game

"Has he done it yet? He's got to get his bum cheeks out in Burton's, hasn't he? You can't break a promise, you've got to go there and do it. It won't be a pretty sight, but who cares? Get your butt cheeks out, Gary! That'll put a few Christmas shoppers off, won't it?"

**Holloway wants Bristol City manager Gary Johnson to go through with his bet of baring his backside in a shop window**

"Look at the prickly little fella down the road at Chelsea. He wants to win everything and we can learn from that. If there were two flies crawling up the wall he'd be desperate to back the winner."

**Holloway on Jose Mourinho**

# CHUFFED AS A BADGER

# REF
# JUSTICE

"It was lucky that the linesman wasn't stood in front of me as I would have poked him with a stick to make sure he was awake. I only hope he has woken up in time for his drive home this evening."

**Holloway isn't impressed with the assistant referee after a QPR loss at Bristol City**

"I was threatened to be arrested for some of my language. There was a policeman stood next to me. I was probably lucky to get away with that."

**The Blackpool manager got very angry during his side's 1-1 draw with Barnsley**

"As far as I'm concerned – I'm from Bristol and so is that lad – and he got it wrong."

**After referee Steve Dunn failed to award a QPR foul for Manchester City's goal**

"When their man was sent off, it seemed to wake up the crowd and give them someone to get their teeth into and fortunately for us that was the referee."

**Holloway after QPR beat 10-man Leicester**

"What the hell the referee saw I don't know – he ought to go to Specsavers."

**The QPR boss slams Lee Probert who gave a last-minute penalty to Sheffield United**

"I've broken them all already! I wasn't gonna swear and I ruined that on New Year's Day by swearing at the fourth official. I was devastated at the end – not because we didn't win the game or that the ref cancelled out our goal or that he should have cancelled their goal or that he sent my centre forward off for deliberate handball which wasn't deliberate at all. Nothing to do with any of that – it was the fact that I swore at the fourth official about the linesman on the other side. So that's one New Year's resolution gone and the second one went that night when I was a bit down and had one glass of wine too many. So what a terrible New Year I'm having! I wasn't going to drink for at least a month and I was going to get fit and all that and I've blown it."

**On his New Year's resolutions**

"We're getting absolutely bo diddley squat, week in, week out. But there you go, such is life."

**The Blackpool manager after his side controversially lost to Manchester City**

"The refereeing was very one-sided but I will take my medicine. I got incensed and said one or two swear words I'm not allowed to say. It's ironic you can get sworn at and intimidated all day and if you show emotion you're in trouble. I'm pleading guilty and I have apologised to the referee. But football is about passion and the day I don't care is the day I give up."

**On the officiating for QPR's draw against Cardiff**

"No-one ever fights for the right thing. We're in Brexit now. None of us knew we had to pay however many million or billion to get out of it, did we? They never gave us that information, so we're out of it now. These referees should have that top man who can't run anymore talking to that very good young referee saying, 'Actually that's not a penalty'. I keep saying, let's make sure we get respect. Retire the people that can't run as fast anymore and sit them with a monitor and let them talk to the referee."

**Holloway compares the refereeing system to Brexit in a bizarre rant after QPR's draw with Bristol City**

"I'm not nice when I don't get what I want. But my mum would have washed my mouth if she had seen what the officials wrote down from what I said to them after Spurs. I've eaten a bar of soap before and then I swear like a trooper!"

**The Palace boss was upset in the dugout**

"We might as well go back to being cavemen, grab our girl by the hair, drag her into the cave whether she wants to come in or not because we may as well live in that age. We've come forward, haven't we?"

**The Blackpool boss wants referees to be able to refer to video footage**

"I would like to keep my money in my pocket and pay for my other daughter's wedding next summer. Come to the pub and I will tell you exactly what I feel. I can't make anything of it because my opinion doesn't count. I've realised that now."

**The Palace boss won't reveal his true feelings on the ref for fear of a fine**

"I have to say I think one of my old favourite cartoon characters Mr Magoo would have seen that."

**Holloway on a Sheffield Wednesday goal after what appeared to be an obvious foul on Plymouth's keeper**

"We judge referees by so many camera angles so people at home eating Doritos and having a beer can see he's wrong."

**The Blackpool manager wants to see video technology introduced**

"I have never seen such a stonewall penalty kick in all my life. Even my wife in St Albans could see that it was a penalty."

**After QPR had a spot kick turned down against Grimsby**

"If that's a penalty, then I may as well say I'm Alec McJockstrap and wear a kilt."

**The Leicester boss is angry at the officials**

# CHUFFED AS A BADGER

# CALL THE MANAGER

"I thought it was Easter Monday by the time he got to the bench. He had a Zimmer frame how slow he was walking."

**The Blackpool boss fumes at the time it took Newcastle's Shola Ameobi to leave the field after being substituted**

"I don't like Ben Foster because he's just ended my dream. I am sick whenever I lose. Just ask my mum what I was like even when I lost at tiddlywinks as a kid. We threw everything we could at them – the kitchen sink, the golf clubs, everything. We emptied the garage and threw it at them – at least my garage is tidy now."

**The Plymouth boss after an inspired display by Watford keeper Ben Foster**

"I wouldn't say kick in the teeth, it feels a lot worse than that. It probably feels like somewhere else, more like the crown jewels."

**Holloway after a Palace defeat**

"After the game, we're walking off the pitch. We've just won 2-1. The ref's given us a goal that was blatantly offside, so I'm absolutely elated. Neil Warnock, the Sheffield United manager, is going ballistic. Anyhow, I am shouting at Neil, as we walk off, 'I always supported you. But now I see I was wrong. Everybody else in football is right. You are a tw*t!'"

**On his managerial rival Warnock**

"I was up and down like Zebedee from the Magic Roundabout. We had a monster team out there, all the big guys, the roof inspectors as I call them."

**Holloway after QPR came back from two goals down to beat Leicester 3-2**

"Richard Langley looked like he was still in Trinidad and Tobago playing for Jamaica. He's got to realise what it's all about. It's not just him, it's all of them, but I'll start with the big ones and work my way down, because that ain't good enough."

**After QPR are shocked by non-league side Vauxhall Motors in an FA Cup replay**

"I lost to Vauxhall Motors in the cup on penalties – now you don't get much more embarrassing than that because their name is atrocious isn't it? It sounded like we were beaten by a car. We didn't get into first gear and were automatically knocked out of the cup. It meant that much that a taxi driver, who is now a good friend of mine, came in and spoke to me for two hours about what I should have done. But then I looked at the team he would have picked and I said, 'They're all bloody injured, you complete pillock'. He didn't realise how hard it was being a football manager."

**Holloway later recalls that infamous Vauxhall Motors defeat**

"We were like the Dog and Duck in the first half and Real Madrid in the second. We can't go on like that. At full time I was at them like an irritated Jack Russell."

**QPR came back from two goals down to draw with Hull**

"I wanted to take Varney off and put Carney on but we ended up taking off Crainey. It all got confused. Varney, Carney, Crainey is a tongue-twister."

**Holloway substituted the wrong Blackpool player against Wolves**

"It's one of my proudest days in football, but I've caught the bouquet again. I'm always the bridesmaid."

**After QPR were defeated in the play-off final**

"Van Basten thought about hitting a shot once and it went in – then 'Reg', what are you doing? Oh, get in! Brilliant."

**On Luke Varney's goal for Blackpool against Wolves**

"Look at the state of Neil Warnock. His head was coming off and quite rightly so."

**The Blackpool boss after Warnock's Palace had a penalty turned down**

"The fat lady hasn't started to sing yet, but she has a mic in her hand."

**Holloway concedes QPR's chances of reaching the play-offs are virtually over**

"I don't pay Danny Shittu to pass the ball. I don't pay him to be pretty, I pay him to defend and be in the right place because he's a big monster. Him and Clarke Carlisle have got to sort their lives out and defend for us."

**He criticises his QPR defensive duo**

"I reckon the ball was travelling at 400mph and I bet it burned the keeper's eyebrows off."

**The QPR manager's view away at Crewe**

"Our substitute didn't have his shirts or pants on. I've had better days."

**Holloway bemoans his luck**

"I couldn't be more chuffed if I were a badger at the start of the mating season."

**He is thrilled after QPR beat Cardiff**

"We looked more like Queens Park Strangers out there."

**After five players made their QPR debuts**

"Well a few of them have had their hair done."

**On how the TV cameras affected his players**

"Whoever that was, I would like to pull his pants down and slap his a*se like I used to do to my kids. Apparently I'm not even allowed to do that anymore otherwise I will have the old health and safety on my back giving it the old 'hello'. The world's gone mad. Tony Blair won the election, so why's he gotta resign? I think the Conservative fella should. If he couldn't win an election with a failing government, or a flailing government, what's the matter with him? Get out you ain't no good. I know we're not talking football... we are aren't we?"

**Holloway responds to a journalist who claimed Danny Shittu was being sold by QPR**

"If is a big word. If I had long hair I could be a rock star."

**When a reporter asked if Tony Thorpe had put away a good opportunity at Bristol City**

"Every time Ipswich crossed into our box I felt I might have to go through a new pair of strides."

**After QPR's 2-2 draw at Portman Road**

"We need a big, ugly defender. If we had one of them we'd have dealt with County's first goal by taking out the ball, the player and the first three rows of seats in the stands."

**Holloway after QPR's encounter with Notts County**

"I'd have put my house, its contents, my entire wardrobe, my undergarments, my socks and my shoes on the fact that he would score. How he didn't, I have no idea."

**On a bad miss by Leicester's Iain Hume**

"If it had been my kids I would have bought them an ice cream ages ago."

**The Blackpool boss believes his fringe players deserved their places against Villa**

"I had a midfield so young they should have been in nappies. It was a debacle."

**The Leicester manager after losing to Southampton in the FA Cup**

"One of their members of staff has been as rude as f*ck about us, so it's about us coming out on top. It's not about pretty football, it's about winning football. We've got to go out today. Let's get on our f*cking toes. Let's get in here. All my life I've been on a crusade because you can be a winner without being rude. Get f*cking focused. Get in nice and tight. Feel that f*cking strength."

**Holloway's pep talk to his players before a QPR win over Brighton**

"There was a spell in the second half when I took my heart off my sleeve and put it in my mouth."

**Holloway after Rangers beat Coventry**

"There was an incident in the second half, when Bobby Zamora dived to get West Ham a free-kick. That was a real splash."

**Holloway on the West Ham striker 'diving'**

"Once we had got the equaliser, I wanted to put jump leads on my players because I thought we had an excellent chance of nicking a win."

**On a missed QPR chance at Forest**

"It was tense and I was dying for the toilet. As soon as Kevin [McLeod] scored, I went."

**Holloway dashed to the bogs after the midfielder's 88th-minute goal in QPR's 2-0 win over Wrexham**

"We're on the crest of a slump but you won't get me criticising the players. I feel like I've been mugged."

**After a Rovers defeat against Preston**

"It's not life threatening, he's gonna be fine, he's not maimed, he's not blown up like any of our heroes in the war."

**The Blackpool manager after Matt Gilks broke his kneecap**

"He over-elaborated with his celebration. He looked like a chicken stick."

**The Hoops boss on Richard Langley's goal celebration**

# CHUFFED AS A BADGER

# SAY THAT AGAIN?

## CHUFFED AS A BADGER

"To put it in gentleman's terms if you've been out for a night and you're looking for a young lady and you pull one, some weeks they're good looking and some weeks they're not the best. Our performance today would have been not the best looking bird but at least we got her in the taxi. She weren't the best looking lady we ended up taking home but she was very pleasant and very nice, so thanks very much, let's have a coffee."

**One of Holloway's most famous post-match comments after a win against Chesterfield**

"If my aunty had balls, she'd be my uncle."

**Holloway on his family**

### Say That Again?

"Without Laurel and Hardy, Laurel wouldn't be Hardy."

**The Palace manager on the comedy duo**

"Promotion would be another notch in my football bedpost."

**Holloway on going up with Palace**

"It's no good counting your chickens. Even if we're 2-0 up with five minutes to go on Saturday don't think we've already done it, we've got to kill it off, hold people down and strangle the life out of them."

**He wants his side to finish teams off**

"It's like the film Men in Black. I walk around in a black suit, white shirt and black tie where I've had to flash my white light every now and again to erase some memories. But I feel we've got hold of the galaxy now. It's in our hands."

**On coping with QPR's financial constraints**

"We've picked the ship up off the bottom of the ocean, plugged a few leaks and we're floating on the top. Now we want to turn around and sail off into the sunset."

**On QPR's achievements over the season**

"My players need to run and make runs."

**The Palace manager has the runs**

### Say That Again?

"I've been polishing that car since I've been here. Unfortunately, I didn't buy it off the forecourt straight away... I'm not going to spend all this time polishing that car and then let somebody rip it away from me off my drive in the summer for absolutely nothing. That's bad business. Somebody is going to have to buy it off me, and I might have to push it off my drive if it doesn't want to go."

**Plymouth boss on the car – Tony Capaldi – who drove off to Cardiff City**

"Now I'm a little fella as it happens, but when I was really small I was nothing."

**He was picked up by Bristol Rovers as a kid**

"You never count your chickens before they hatch. I used to keep parakeets and I never counted every egg thinking I would get all eight birds. You just hoped they came out of the nest box looking all right."

**When asked if QPR can get automatically promoted**

"It's all very well having a great pianist playing but it's no good if you haven't got anyone to get the piano on the stage in the first place, otherwise the pianist would be standing there with no bloody piano to play."

**Holloway on his limited Leicester squad**

## Say That Again?

"Who would have thought a few weeks ago that we would be sitting in this position now? It's like the song, 'Wait a minute, it stopped hailing, guys are swimming, gals are sailing'. I love that song."

**Holloway on the Hoops being in the top half of the table**

"If you can keep your noses in front at the end, that's what counts. It's been said that I have a bit of a Roman nose and I am keeping it ahead at the moment. Hopefully it's all about the length of your hooter because I might be in front at the end of the season as well!"

**After QPR's win over Brighton**

"Every dog has its day – and today is woof day! Today I just want to bark."

**Holloway on QPR's promotion-winning victory at Sheffield Wednesday**

"The trouble with us is that we've had too many players sitting at the piano, not moving it."

**The Rovers boss laments his side's lack of quality despite beating Bristol City**

"You can say that strikers are a bit like postmen, they have to get in and out as quick as they can before the dog has a go."

**Holloway on his forwards**

### Say That Again?

"We are an offshoot of apes – allegedly – but who knows? We don't really, do we? How long have we been on this planet? How long are we going to be here? What is it all about? We reproduce. Our offspring carry on. Before the whole thing blows up and we are sucked into a black hole. You know what I mean?"

**Holloway the nature enthusiast**

"As long as you hit the target they go in, if the keeper don't make a save."

**The manager stating the obvious**

"Sometimes when you aim for the stars, you hit the moon."

**Holloway on his Leicester forward line**

"We've got a good squad and we're going to cut our cloth accordingly, but I think the cloth that we've got could make some good soup, if that makes any sense."

**On working with a small squad**

"When you play with wingers you look a bit like a taxi with both doors open, anyone can get in or out."

**Holloway is not happy with a Rangers pre-season friendly result**

## Say That Again?

"We've got to go there and tweak the nose of fear and stick an ice cube down the vest of terror. That's not an Ian Holloway quote, by the way. It's Blackadder."

**The Leicester boss before a crunch clash against Stoke**

"If you're a burglar, it's no good poncing about outside somebody's house, looking good with your swag bag ready. Just get in there, burgle them and come out. I don't advocate that obviously, it's just an analogy."

**On Blackpool's chances of winning the play-offs after losing to Palace**

"I always say that scoring goals is like driving a car. When the striker is going for goal, he's pushing down that accelerator, so the rest of the team has to come off that clutch. If the clutch and the accelerator are down at the same time, then you are going to have an accident."

**Holloway is driving himself crazy about his strike-force**

"Right now, everything is going wrong for me – if I fell in a barrel of boobs, I'd come out sucking my thumb!"

**Holloway bemoans his bad run of luck while with Rangers**

## Say That Again?

"Everyone wants a bag of carrots, and they might be a bag of carrots, if you know what I mean."

**The Blackpool manager gives food for thought on transfer deadline day**

"If anyone is counting their chickens, they haven't hatched out yet. You can look at the eggs, but you don't know how many chickens you're going to get, so we'll just sit in there and have a go."

**The Palace boss, who loves a 'chicken and egg' analogy is not getting complacent**

"I'm like a swan at the moment. I look fine on top of the water but under the water my little legs are going mad."

**Holloway after QPR beat Bristol City**

"Front line did, the back line did it and they got through us. And my back line did opposite to my middle line. I mean I could have scored that, it's just ridiculous."

**The Palace boss gets all tactical**

"It's like putting a snake in a bag, if you don't tie it up, it will wriggle free."

**Holloway hails the spirit of his QPR players after they rescued a point against Millwall**

"That emperor's got no clothes on; he's absolutely butt naked."

**The Blackpool manager loves a metaphor**

"When the water stands still in the pond, it starts to stink."

**Holloway on dropping his QPR players**

"This is a feather in our cap. It's there in our pocket."

**The Palace manager confuses us**

"I want you to bad rash them."

**During a pre-match team talk on BBC Radio**

# Also available

Printed in Great Britain
by Amazon

11915380R00078